We Can Do It!

HOUGHTON MIFFLIN   BOSTON • MORRIS PLAINS, NJ

California • Colorado • Georgia • Illinois • New Jersey • Texas

ISBN 0-618-07501-1

6789-BS-06 05 04 03 02

Design, Art Management, and Page Production: Studio Goodwin Sturges

Contents

Sport Gets a Bath

by Pat Brennan
illustrated by Diane Palmisciano

"Good morning, Kim," said
Norm. "What's under the
porch? I hear snoring!"

"It's my dog, Sport!" sighed
Kim. "She is sleeping in the
dirt."

"Sport's fur is full of dirt!" said Kim. "She needs a bath now."

"That's a big chore, but we can do it," said Norm.

"Squeeze her firmly, Norm.
I'll squirt the hose," said Kim.
"Sport will be cleaner than
ever!"

"Help!" yelled Norm. "You squirted me. Sport is dry, but my shirt is wet!"

"Oops!" blurted Kim. "The hose twirled around."

"Look at Sport now. Her fur
isn't black at all. Her fur is
yellow!" said Norm.

"No, Sport!" shouted Kim.
"Don't shake! My skirt is
soaked!"

"Look, Mom," cried Kim. "We gave Sport a bath. She had dirt all over herself."

"Sport looks good," said Mom, "but who is more wet? Is it Sport or you and Norm?"

Home Run

by Patrick Bracken
illustrated by Paul Meisel

"Can you play this morning, Sam?" asked Kirk.

"Yes," said Sam. "I'll bring Jane, too. I will teach her a new sport."

The kids began to play. Kirk's team scored three runs. Sam's team scored three runs, too. The game was tied.

It was Jane's turn at bat. Her
team needed one more run.
Everyone knew Jane could not
score.

Jane got a big hit! She ran to
first base. Kirk threw to get her
out. He threw too high! It went
over a boy's head at first base.

Jane ran to second base.
Again, Kirk's team threw. This
time it went over a girl at second
base. Jane ran to third base!

Sam yelled, "Stay at third base."

The team shouted, "Run home, Jane. Run home!"

Jane tore off.

"She's going home, just like you said!" smiled Sam. "That's really a home run!"

Pet Store

by Eileen McGaferty
illustrated by Renée Andriani

"Look, Dad!" cried Jake. "It's a pet store. Can we go inside?"

"Why not?" smiled Dad. "We can make one more stop before we go home."

Inside, Jake saw lots of tanks
and cages with all sorts of pets
in them. Jake did not know
where to turn first!

The first pet Jake saw was a big
blue bird on a perch. This bird
made Jake laugh. It didn't chirp.
It squawked, "Good morning!"

The second pet Jake saw was
a green and yellow bird with
spots on its head. This bird used
its beak to break open nuts.

Then Jake saw a cat with soft
gray fur. It purred when it saw
Jake and Dad.

Just then, the store clerk came by.

"There is one more thing you must see!" she said.

"These pups were born this morning," said the clerk. She pointed out five sleeping pups curled up by their mom.

"Wow!" Jake shouted. "This is the best thing I've seen all week!"

Big Star's Gifts

by Pat Brennan
illustrated by Marlene McDonald

Barb woke up. She got out
of bed and looked outside.
Her whole yard was snowy!

Barb got dressed quickly.
Then she ran to the back yard.
She picked a place to make her
snowman. Then she got started.
She worked hard all morning.

Barb's hard work paid off.
Her piles of snow started to look
like a real snowman. The hard
part of her job was done.

Now came the fun part. Barb
made a face out of big dark
prunes. She used sharp sticks
to make arms.

Barb tied a red scarf on the snowman's neck. She placed a cap on his head. Then she gave the snowman a name. She named him Big Star.

For days, Big Star stood
smiling in Barb's yard. Then one
day he melted. But he left gifts
in Barb's yard.

Here is what Big Star left for Barb.

Car Trip

by Eileen McGaferty
illustrated by Daniel Clifford

Art's family piled in the car.
They were going to Gram's farm.
It was far. Dad started to drive.

Dad stopped at a pay booth.
He stretched out his arm and
threw in coins.

"Are we at Gram's yet?" asked
Art.

"We've hardly started," Meg laughed.

As Dad drove, Meg and Art saw lots of farms and barns.

"Are we at Gram's yet?" asked Art.

Dad stopped at a park to eat, rest, and play. Art ran and ran. At last Meg caught him. Then it was back in the car.

The sun started to set. Soon
it was dark. Meg and Art saw
stars above them in the night
sky. Art leaned on Meg.

"Are we at Gram's yet?"
he asked.

Meg had an idea.

"I will tell you clues," said
Meg. "You name the animal on
the card."

They played and played.

42

Then Mom yelled, "We are
at Gram's now!"

"Already?" asked Art.

And Mom, Dad, and Meg
laughed hard.

Mark's Part

by Pat Brennan
illustrated by John Nez

"Mom, Mom!" shouted Mark.
"I got a part in the class play!"

Mark showed Mom his dark
cape. He would wear it when
he marched on stage.

"Mom, how will you know me?"
he asked. "Five other kids have
dark capes, too."

Mom said, "I am smart enough
to spot my own boy."

The next day, Mark went
skating in Green Hill Park. A
dog was barking at a bird and
darted right into Mark. Mark
fell hard against the ground.

Mark felt a sharp pain in his arm. Soon Mark's arm was in a cast.

At last the big day came.
Mom went to see Mark play
his part. The lights went out
and it was time to begin.

Six kids in dark capes marched on stage. Mom saw Mark right away. She waved and clapped hard. Mark felt like a star!

Ice-Cold Drinks

by Patrick Bracken
illustrated by Tricia Tusa

Rose and Bruce set up a selling stand. Bruce wrote this:

Ice-cold drinks for sale.

Sweetest, coolest drinks in town! Just ten cents!

Rose and Bruce waited. But
no one came for drinks.

"Maybe it needs to be
sweeter," said Bruce.

So Rose made the drinks
sweeter.

But still no one came for drinks.

"Maybe it needs to be cooler," said Rose.

So Bruce made the drinks cooler.

But still no one came for
drinks.

Rose yelled, "Come and get
your ice-cold drinks!"

But still no one came for
drinks.

Bruce said, "Maybe you need
to yell louder."

So Rose yelled louder.

But still no one came for drinks.

"Maybe we need to make the price lower," said Rose.

So Bruce made the price lower.

Soon lots of people came by.
Everyone wanted the sweetest,
coolest, lowest-priced drinks
in town.

The Best Pie

by Patrick Bracken
illustrated by Rebecca Bond

Miss Cook, Miss Bake, and Miss Sweet saw an ad. It said: Who makes the sweetest, lightest, moistest pie in town? Bring your pies to the pie feast and find out!

The three friends had the same thoughts.

"We are each able to bake pies," said Miss Cook. "We can bake for the pie feast."

Miss Cook ran home. She got
her biggest bowl and started
mixing. Then she took a bite.

"It needs to be sweeter,"
she said.

Then she added sweet spices.

Miss Bake ran home. She
mixed the pie filling. She took
a bite.

"It needs to be lighter," she
said.

Then she added an egg.

Miss Sweet ran home. She mixed and mixed, too. She took a bite.

"It needs to be moister," she said.

Then she added more milk.

At the pie feast, Sam tested each pie. He tied a scarf over his eyes and took a bite from each pie.

Which pie will win?

Miss Cook, Miss Bake, and
Miss Sweet each got a first-prize
present—new shirts!

Don't Ask Me

by Eileen McGaferty
illustrated by Kathryn Mitter

"Happy birthday, Marge!" said
Mom. "Did Dad tell you where
we are going?"

"Not yet!" blurted Marge.

"We are going to Fred's
farm," laughed Dad.

Marge saw four new pups
at Fred's farm.

"This brown and white pup is
the runt," said Farmer Fred.
"It's the smallest. That pup
with black spots is the biggest."

"That pup with patches on its eyes jumps highest," he added. "This pup with white paws runs the fastest. Which pup do you like?"

Each pup was softer and
sweeter than the next.

"Don't ask me," sighed Marge.
"It's too hard to choose."

"Let's let a pup choose you,"
said Dad.

As Dad and Marge stepped
back, the shortest pup jumped
up. It ran after Marge, wagging
its tail.

The pup wagged its tail faster
and licked Marge's hand.

"I choose the pup that chose
me," laughed Marge.

Now Marge has a pup named
Zoom. Zoom is the cutest,
sweetest, nicest dog around.
Just ask Marge!

Word Lists

Theme 10, Week 1

Sport Gets a Bath (p. 5) accompanies *Two Greedy Bears*.

Decodable Words

New

r-Controlled Vowels *or, ore:* *morning, Norm, or, porch, snoring, Sport, Sport's, chore, more*

r-Controlled Vowels *er, ir, ur:* *cleaner, ever, her, herself, under, dirt, firmly, shirt, skirt, squirt, squirted, twirled, blurted, fur*

Previously Taught

and, at, bath, be, big, black, but, cried, dog, dry, gave, gets, good, had, help, hose, in, is, isn't, it's, Kim, look, looks, me, Mom, my, needs, no, now, oops, shake, she, shouted, sighed, sleeping, soaked, squeeze, than, that's, we, wet, will, yelled, yellow, you

High-Frequency Words

Previously Taught

a, all, around, don't, full, hear, I, I'll, of, over, said, the, what's, who

Theme 10, Week 1

Home Run (p. 13) accompanies *Two Greedy Bears*.

Decodable Words

New

r-Controlled Vowels *or, ore:* *morning, sport, more, score, scored, tore*

r-Controlled Vowels *er, ir, ur:* *her, first, girl, Kirk, Kirk's, third, turn*

Previously Taught

asked, at, base, bat, big, boy's, bring, but, can, game, get, going, got, he, high, hit, home, it, Jane, Jane's, just, kids, knew, like, needed, new, not, out, play, ran, really, run, runs, Sam, Sam's, she, she's, shouted, smiled, stay, teach, team, that's, this, three, threw, tied, time, too, went, will, yelled, yes, you

High-Frequency Words

New

began, second

Previously Taught

a, again, could, everyone, head, I, I'll, off, one, over, said, the, to, was

Theme 10, Week 1

Pet Store (p. 21) accompanies *Two Greedy Bears.*

Decodable Words

New
<u>r-Controlled Vowels *or, ore:*</u> *born, morning, sorts, before, more, store*

<u>r-Controlled Vowels *er, ir, ur:*</u> *clerk, perch, bird, chirp, first, curled, fur, purred, turn*

Previously Taught
and, beak, best, big, blue, by, cages, came, can, cat, cried, Dad, did, didn't, five, go, good, gray, green, home, in, inside, is, it, its, it's, Jake, just, know, look, lots, made, make, mom, must, not, nuts, on, out, pet, pets, pointed, pups, saw, see, seen, she, shouted, sleeping, smiled, soft, spots, squawked, stop, tanks, them, then, these, thing, this, up, used, we, week, when, why, with, wow, yellow, you

High-Frequency Words

New
break, head, laugh, second

Previously Taught
a, all, I've, of, one, open, said, the, their, there, to, was, were, where

Theme 10, Week 2

Big Star's Gifts (p. 29) accompanies *Fireflies for Nathan.*

Decodable Words

New
<u>r-Controlled Vowels *ar:*</u> *arms, Barb, Barb's, dark, hard, part, scarf, sharp, Star, Star's, started, yard*

Previously Taught
and, back, bed, big, but, came, cap, day, days, dressed, face, for, fun, gave, gifts, got, he, her, him, his, in, is, job, left, like, look, looked, made, make, melted, morning, name, named, neck, now, on, out, outside, paid, picked, piles, place, placed, prunes, quickly, ran, real, red, she, smiling, snow, snowman, snowman's, snowy, sticks, stood, then, tied, up, used, whole, woke

High-Frequency Words

Previously Taught
a, all, done, head, here, of, off, one, the, to, was, what, work, worked

Theme 10, Week 2

Car Trip (p. 37) accompanies *Fireflies for Nathan.*

Decodable Words

New
<u>r-Controlled Vowels *ar:*</u> *arm, Art, Art's, barns, car, card, dark, far, farm, farms, hard, hardly, park, stars, started*

Previously Taught
an, and, as, asked, at, back, booth, clues, coins, Dad, drive, drove, eat, going, Gram's, had, he, him, his, in, it, last, leaned, lots, Meg, Mom, name, night, now, on, out, pay, piled, play, played, ran, rest, saw, set, sky, soon, stopped, stretched, sun, tell, them, then, threw, trip, we, we've, will, yelled, yet, you

High-Frequency Words

New
above, already, caught

Previously Taught
a, animal, are, family, I, idea, laughed, of, said, the, they, to, was, were

Theme 10, Week 2

Mark's Part (p. 45) accompanies *Fireflies for Nathan.*

Decodable Words

New
<u>r-Controlled Vowels *ar:*</u> *arm, barking, dark, darted, hard, marched, Mark, Mark's, Park, part, sharp, smart, star*

Previously Taught
am, and, asked, at, big, bird, boy, came, cape, capes, cast, clapped, class, day, dog, fell, felt, five, got, Green, ground, he, Hill, his, how, in,

78

(*Mark's Part*, Previously Taught Decodable Words continued)

it, kids, know, last, lights, like, me, Mom, my, next, on, out, own, pain, play, right, saw, see, she, shouted, showed, six, skating, soon, spot, stage, time, too, waved, went, when, will, you

High-Frequency Words

New
against, begin

Previously Taught
a, away, enough, have, I, into, other, said, the, to, was, wear, would

Theme 10, Week 3

Ice-Cold Drinks (p. 53) accompanies *The Hat*.

Decodable Words

New
Base Words and Endings -er, -est: *cooler, louder, lower, sweeter, coolest, lowest, sweetest*

Previously Taught
and, be, Bruce, but, by, came, cents, drinks, for, get, in, it, just, lots, made, make, maybe, need, needs, no, price, priced, Rose, sale, selling, set, so, soon, stand, still, ten, this, town, up, waited, we, wrote, yell, yelled, you

High-Frequency Words

Previously Taught
a, come, everyone, ice-cold, of, one, people, said, the, to, wanted, your

Theme 10, Week 3

The Best Pie (p. 61) accompanies *The Hat*.

Decodable Words

New
Base Words and Endings -er, -est: *lighter, moister, biggest, lightest, moistest, sweetest*

(*The Best Pie*, Decodable Words continued)

Previously Taught
ad, added, an, and, at, Bake, be, best, bite, bowl, bring, can, Cook, each, egg, feast, filling, first-prize, for, from, got, had, he, her, his, home, in, it, makes, milk, Miss, mixed, mixing, more, needs, new, out, pie, pies, ran, Sam, same, saw, scarf, she, shirts, spices, started, Sweet, tested, then, three, tied, too, took, town, we, which, will, win

High-Frequency Words

New
eyes, present, thoughts

Previously Taught
a, able, are, find, friends, over, said, the, to, who, your

Theme 10, Week 3

Don't Ask Me (p. 69) accompanies *The Hat*.

Decodable Words

New
Base Words and Endings -er, -est: *faster, softer, sweeter, biggest, cutest, fastest, highest, nicest, shortest, sweetest*

Previously Taught
added, and, as, ask, at, back, birthday, black, blurted, brown, choose, chose, Dad, did, dog, each, farm, farmer, Fred, Fred's, going, hand, happy, hard, has, he, is, it, its, it's, jumped, jumps, just, let, let's, licked, like, Marge, Marge's, me, Mom, named, new, next, not, now, on, patches, paws, pup, pups, ran, runs, runt, saw, sighed, spots, stepped, tail, tell, than, that, this, too, up, wagged, wagging, we, which, white, with, yet, you, Zoom

High-Frequency Words

New
eyes

Previously Taught
a, after, are, around, do, don't, four, I, laughed, said, smallest, the, to, was, where